WOMEN IN BUSINESS

THE ONE ALL BUSINESSMEN SHOULD READ (BUT PROBABLY WON'T)

ADAM DAVISON & CULAIN WOOD

CONTENTS

AUTHOR'S NOTE

This book, the first in a series of books from Trinity U, has been researched and written through the partnership of Adam Davison and Culain Wood.

Adam is the founder and owner of Trinity U, whilst Culain is a writer and owner of Wood With Words.

The anecdotes in the book are all real-life accounts of women that Adam has recorded podcasts with.

These stories have then been interpreted into writing by Culain.

The analysis has been done in partnership, and at each stage of testing and drafting, the two have collaborated, reflected and responded as a team.

The original podcast material was researched and recorded by Adam Davison.

The written content was interpreted and produced by Culain Wood.

All words and content are the property of the authors.

INTRODUCTION

A time will come when the world will have no need for books specifically about 'women in this' and 'women in that', as we will eventually reach a point where we simply talk about 'people in this' and 'people in that'.

Sadly though, we're not there yet…

"In the United Kingdom, among the companies in the FTSE 100 index, women hold 22.8% of board seats…"

That's less than a quarter. We're clearly not there yet.

In fact, with issues such as gender pay inequality and sexual harassment in the workplace, there really is a long way to go until we can confine books like this to the history section.

Not that they should ever be forgotten of course, because where you've come from is always important when telling your story, but at TrinityU, we believe that where you're heading is even more important.

That's why this, the first of our series of books all about real people in business, focuses solely on females in the business world.

Based on real conversations it tells their stories, acknowledges their struggles and celebrates their successes.

Ultimately, we want to shine a light on their business stories full stop, not their business stories simply because they are women, and we hope that grouping this collection of case studies together will serve as a reminder that gender is no limitation to succeeding in business.

The accounts from this point onwards, are all accounts of real women with real businesses. Their stories are unique to them, but there are similarities in their struggles and successes. We listen to their stories first, as they are the most important thing, before pulling out any key bits of analysis or relevant themes.

Women in Business, this is how it's done.

Men in Business, all this learning applies to you too...

1

THE ONE WITH THE FITNESS PROFESSIONAL. "I WAS TERRIFIED..."

How many times do we hear a story about a hugely successful businessperson, that starts with them leaving school at 16? Quite often!

Many people in business start off on their journey to business success by stepping away from the academic route and entering the world of work as soon as they are legally allowed to. Many jump into the world of work before this too, and an entrepreneurial spirit can be hard to contain.

Trying a little bit of this, and a little bit of that often leads a person to discovering their calling, one way or another.

Now whilst the first of our 'women in business', K as we will call her, did eventually find her calling and build her business, it would be fair to say that she spent a fair bit of time wondering what to do, and giving different things a try. A childhood dream of wanting to be a professional dancer didn't work out as she had planned, leading to a stint in retail, closely followed by a role as a secretary at an accountancy firm.

These early entries to the CV may seem a world away from her eventual business life as a fitness professional, but that's sort of the point.

Every journey is unique and every experience, good or bad, helps us get there.

Following a few years working as a receptionist at a TV company in Manchester, which she loved, K was forced to deal with redundancy, all before turning 20 years old too. With £800 in her pocket, and not much of an idea about what to do with it, she sought advice from her dad, who gave her a nudge back towards following her dreams.

Well, sort of.

K trained to become an aerobics instructor, with the words "you might enjoy it..." ringing in her ears. Eight years later, she had influenced the lives of so many people through her classes and coaching, showing that sometimes, going with your gut feeling can really pay off.

Now, whilst K may well have helped a lot of people in that period of time, it's also true to say that she worked hard to upskill herself and gain qualification on top of qualification. A commitment to personal and professional development like this is something that every single person, whether they're in business or not, could benefit from.

Intrinsic motivation and admirable dedication allowed K to become a gym instructor in this time, along with gaining a whole load of other industry specific qualifications and accreditations.

Alongside running her own classes, in the way she thought best at the time, she began working for the NHS, in Health Improvement. Her passion for helping people become the best version of themselves extended to areas such as dietary advice, how to stop smoking and how to increase physical activity.

An ever-widening skillset and a vast array of experiences, all by the age of 25.

But no academic qualification.

Whilst this isn't always a barrier to succeeding in business, an academic qualification can open certain doors that an individual might not have even knew existed. A BSc in Physical Activity

and Health Sciences dove tailed perfectly into K's existing experience, and so for three years, she threw herself into the degree, and by her own admission she absolutely loved it.

There's a real theme emerging here with K's story, one of positivity and loving life. This enthusiasm and energy go such a long way when it comes to making it in business, as it places a value on enjoying the here and now, instead of worrying about what comes next or where it all leads.

As it happens, K hadn't quite figured that out...

Graduating whilst pregnant, she was forced to rethink her exit strategy from university, as a role she had hoped to apply for simply didn't fit with her next steps. Eventually, voluntary redundancies came about within the NHS, and K took the package, knowing that her degree, combined with her experience would help her do something, even if she didn't quite know what that 'something' would be.

K didn't have a plan but was curious to see what would happen next for her.

Not having a plan isn't always the worst thing you can do, and serendipity is still a thing in the big bad twenty first century, but on the back of two redundancies, a degree and a brand-new baby, K's lack of a plan led her down a road she probably wouldn't have intended to go down.

Working for a charity, it suddenly dawned on her that she was doing all of this hard work, commuting such a long way there and back, and not seeing her child as much as she wanted, but she was doing it all for other people. K was still teaching her classes around the day job too, and she just needed to stop and ask herself the question...

"Why am I doing this?"

And just like that, she set her business up in 2014, with just four personal training clients on the books, and a child just about to start school.

Sometimes the hard way is the only way. It's worth reminding ourselves that this point in the journey came off the back of two redundancies, a degree, a child and then the notion of 'jacking it all in...'

Brave, or stupid? That's what most people would ask, and K herself admits to being terrified about what would come next.

What did come next wasn't ideal, as a mortgage payment bounced, and her new little family endured what K calls a 'hairy few months.'

This would've been enough to send a few people back to the day job, but despite all of the challenges, she was incredibly excited as well. K knew that she could do something amazing, and so she set to work on achieving just that.

So, how do you set to work on building a business, when you've never done that before? It isn't easy, and K soon realised that making it up as she went along would only get her so far.

The systems and processes that help businesses succeed are not inherent and not necessarily intuitive either, or as we always say, you don't know what you don't know...

Booking systems, software, plus a whole host of things that she hadn't even considered would be essential; it all started to mount up and cloud the really enjoyable side of things, the stuff she was already good at. K was, and is, an outstanding personal trainer, who didn't really know too much about business.

The iceberg analogy is useful here, in that the 20% we can see, the bit above the water, is K doing her job, helping people reach their goals. But the 80% we can't see, the largest part of the iceberg, is hidden beneath the surface. This is the nitty gritty of running a business. Accounts, health & safety, marketing, the list goes on.

Fast forward six years and the business is continuing to go from strength to strength. So, what about the 80%? How did K manage it? Well, she had a plethora of successful individuals to look up to. Inspirations and role models are crucial, just as coaches are.

Yes, even coaches need coaches!

It took some time and a lot of patience, even a few mistakes along the way, but managing the business, as opposed to doing the job, was something that K needed to get to grips with, and she did. Outsourcing, delegation, sharing the load, It's never easy when it's your baby, your business, but sometimes, it's absolutely necessary.

K's story is one that has plenty of pitfalls and false starts, but the positives of reaching this point in business make it all more than worth it.

She lists the main positives of running her own business as being able to spend more time with her child and being more flexible with when and how she works. These may seem like simple pleasures, and that's absolutely true, but the simple things in life are often what make it worth living.

Control of her workload, control of her work/ life balance, control over the hours she works. All of these things have been achieved through hard work, patience and crucially, seeking the right advice at the right time, about things that someone brand new to business, simply would not know.

Has anything been sacrificed from the original vision?

Absolutely not, because when all's said and done, K considers herself privileged that she is

able to...

..." work with incredible people on their health and fitness journeys."

And that's what she continues to do, work with her clients. Clients who use her services, clients who know, like and trust her, clients who need her.

She talks about her life in business with such pride, but also acknowledges that there have been times, crucial times at that, where an external 'push' has forced her to take a step she didn't necessarily feel ready to take.

Yes, it's been scary, but it's all about feeling the fear but doing it anyway, and that's what K has done. She may have been terrified at times but look at where she is now and tell us that it wasn't worth it.

The owner of a successful fitness company, and the owner of a successful martial arts training company to boot.

You simply can't tell us it wasn't worth it, can you?

ANALYSIS & THEMES

'Feel the Fear' – At Trinity U, we're big believers in the idea that we should all, from time to time, feel the fear and do it anyway, which is exactly what K did when she left school.

With no real idea as to what she wanted to do, K 'jumped', and though it may have taken her a little while to land on all fours, the experiences she picked up on her journey undoubtedly played a significant part in determining just how far she would go. We're not saying that sliding down the evacuation slide from the education system at the earliest possible juncture is for everyone, of course we're not. We're simply highlighting that the unconventional route, the one that seems the scariest, can sometimes be the most prosperous.

Lifelong learning – By the age of 25, K had built up an impressive collection of qualifications and experiences, which any fitness professional would look back on with pride, even at the end of their career. To say that all of these vocational qualifications were backed up by an academic qualification, is testament to the sheer enthusiasm and dedication she had poured into developing herself through learning. You don't have to go to university to continue your learning, we're not saying that, but viewing your learning journey as constant, rather than with a beginning and an end, will help fuel your desire to absorb new knowledge and experience new things. As K points out, this can only strengthen you in business.

Reflection – Reflection is key to all persons and all situations. It is where we evaluate what went well, and accept what might've been better, before making a plan for our next steps. Sometimes reflection happens with others, for example in appraisals, annual reviews and target meetings, but we find that the reflection we do on our own, irrespective of whether we ever share that with anyone, can be the most useful reflection of all. Why? Because we can be our own harshest critics, and if we can't be honest with ourselves, who can we be honest with? When K stopped and asked herself the question, 'why am I doing this?' she made the first steps to stepping off the hamster wheel and regaining control of her life.

Work/ Life Balance – OK, we know that the concept of any kind of work/ life balance can be an alien proposition for many business owners out there, but when all's said and done, this is surely what we are all striving for. Whether it's the freedom to be able to play golf in the middle of the week, or never having to miss a bedtime story ever again, we're all walking the tightrope between too much work and not enough time for ourselves, our families and our friends. K eventually managed to work her balance out, and she now benefits from what she would consider to be an 'ideal' work/ life balance. As you will have read though, this doesn't happen overnight, it has to be worked towards, but it is achievable. So, keep going!

COMMENTARY - A WORD FROM ADAM DAVISON

"The first thing I reflect on this conversation was her searing honesty when talking about her life and her struggles. To talk so openly about all these area takes so much courage, and, in my experience, it is one area women in business excel at. Openness to talk through the downtimes, to learn from them and then to use them as a steppingstone to the next progression in their life.

Looking back, I can see that the formative years in her life, and all the events during those times, have caused self-doubt and left her with that nagging self-criticism. Learning how to overcome them has meant she can take that experience into her business and allow her clients to benefit from what she has learned.

The road though, will still have twists and turns in it. The past will give her some learnings to call upon, but the drive and determination will be needed as her new business develops and evolves over the coming years and months.

This short story also demonstrates that setting up any business is hard work. Nothing comes easily, but with perseverance, dedication and support you can build a business that will give you the life you desire."

2

THE ONE WITH THE ADMIN AND MARKETING LADY. "IT TOOK ME BACK TO MY WHY?"

When we set up as a new business, or as business owners for the first time, it can have a lot to do with the need to find ourselves again. The world of work can be so draining and demanding that we often lose sight of not just what we want, but who we are. This shouldn't shock everyone into some kind of existential crisis though, as it's perfectly normal to feel like this from time to time.

Our next 'woman in business' felt like this for a few different reasons, and whilst her route to successful business has certainly been fast paced, it definitely hasn't been easy.

KB wasn't just a woman in business, she was a woman with two businesses, a cake making company and an outsourced administration and marketing company. Chalk and cheese to most people maybe, but to her, this was the best use of her varied skillset.

KB is an excellent baker and cake maker, and she is also incredibly skilled when it comes to administration and marketing. So, there we have it. Multitalented and multitasking.

Which is all well and good until the weight shifts from one place to another, and you find yourself trying to strike a balance between the two businesses. It's not easy, as KB found out.

The main focus of the admin and marketing business, is to allow business owners the space to work on their business, rather than in it, giving them time to grow.

Ironically, KB wasn't giving herself much time to grow her own businesses, as she was working incredibly hard to meet the demands of the cake orders. The price of success? Possibly, but working all hours was not what KB had wanted, and it certainly wasn't what her little girl needed.

It was time for her to flip the switch on her businesses, and to reallocate her time in terms of which business took priority.

Why?

Because her priorities changed. She realised that she wasn't able to spend as much time with her little girl as she wanted to with the pressures of cake making. Ultimately, concentrating more on business support took KB back to her 'why'. That 'why' was, and is, her daughter, and she is in no doubt about who motivates her, who keeps her going and who keeps her grounded.

It's all about the 'why', and the business support work allows her to take care of that 'why'.

This all sounds so simple, just making the decision to change focus and watching it all fall into place nice and comfortably. Of course, this doesn't just happen, and there are a number of factors which allow such a transition to take place.

Firstly, KB acknowledges that no matter how hard it gets, no matter the obstacle, her 'why' allows her to keep on moving forward. That's a pretty powerful motivator, and it has clearly fuelled her from strength to strength.

But there is a more practical side to things. As much as we'd love to go with the mantra of 'if you believe, you will achieve' or 'you can do anything if you set your mind to it', there are practical things which must be addressed if these proverbs are ever going to become reality.

For KB, that initially meant looking at building on her client base. How did she do this? Well, there was no 'Oh my Gosh' moment for her, as she already had a network of business associates who knew what KB was about and were happy to entrust her with their outsourced marketing and administration.

The power of networking right there.

Her existing clients continued to use her services, and new clients came aboard at a rapid pace, as they saw the value of her services for themselves.

Incredibly, after just three months, her business was in a position she had hoped it might get to over a period of 18 months. Talk about smashing your goals!

Was this pure luck? Being in the right place at the right time?

Absolutely not. This was down to KB's relationship building skills and appreciation of the value of networking. Basically, it all comes down to ethics.

KB cites ethics and ethos as being the two most important things in business, as they allow everyone involved, stakeholders on every side of the arrangement, to see where things are going and why. This is how trust is formed, when a business's ethos is clear for all to see.

Saying you will do something, saying you will do it a certain way, and then actually doing it. Her ethos centres on enjoying working with people who help people, and that's what she tries to do.

Whether it's health and wellness professionals helping people achieve the body of their dreams, business coaches helping people find the right support, or estate agents helping people find their forever home, it's all about helping those who help others.

This is just another example of KB furthering her understanding of her business, in that she has refined her customer avatar, time and time again, until it is fine-tuned enough to sit perfectly with her ethics and ethos for the business. It works for KB and it gives her job satisfaction.

"Enjoy what you do, and you'll never work a day in your life..."

OK, it still feels like work sometimes, because it can be hard, but at times like that, she is able to look to her clients and realise that in helping them, she is renewing her desire to continue. Refreshing her motivation and remembering her 'why' in the process.

The future looks promising, with more growth on the horizon and the prospect of bringing someone else into the fold. Someone who shares the ethos of the business and of KB herself.

Because not everyone gets 'into business' for the money. Not everyone chooses to step off the payroll and go it alone for selfish reasons. Her motivations were not selfish at all. Wanting to help people was the main motivator.

Stemming from a negative experience KB herself went through, leading up to, during and following the birth of her child, she swore that she would do anything they could to prevent others from feeling how she was made to feel. Whether they've recently had a baby, been poorly, or even made redundant, KB sees her business as a vehicle to provide support and care to anyone, helping them get their businesses where they want them to go. For this reason, she continues to work with clients who she describes as 'genuine, likeminded people, with common ground.'

Powerful stuff.

ANALYSIS & THEMES

Priorities – As small business owners, we can often get sucked into the narrative that we have to be superhuman, all knowing, all seeing and all doing, at all times. We juggle so many balls that the perception of how well we're handling things, is often very different to the reality of how things are going. The unseen work, behind the scenes, can take its toll on anyone. For KB, juggling two businesses and keeping them at the top of their game, was beginning to prove too much, not because they couldn't do it, but because her priorities changed. Our priorities change all the time, and we should never apologise for this. Being aware of what is important to us, at the present time and into the future, is so important in business, as it helps influence decision making and, ultimately, our happiness.

The Power of Networking – We would always advise anyone setting up in business, to get out there into the world of networking. After all, 'it's not the strength of the wolf, it's the strength of the pack,' and in the world of business, having allies can prove so vital at the most unexpected of times. KB is a hard worker, intelligent and talented across several disciplines, but she's also humble enough to appreciate that the strength of her existing network, gave her a brilliant platform from which to set out her targets, and then smash right through them. Without a team around you, who are able to vouch for you, refer you and back you up, the mountain can often feel a lot bigger than it actually is.

Know Your Ethos – Being true to yourself, and to your vision and values, is absolutely key to building integrity and trust in the world of business. You may end up closing off certain areas of the market because they don't necessarily align with your ethics and interpretation of the world, but if you are not willing to accept anything but exactly what you're looking for, then you simply have to stick to your guns. Eventually, the integrity that you have forged out of this consistency and clarity, as long as you deliver what you say you'll deliver, will have your business going from strength to strength because of your ethos, not despite it. KB's overwhelmingly positive ethos of wanting to "help businesses who help people" has almost become her USP, all whilst allowing her to stay true to herself.

Enjoy What You Do– Idealistic, simplistic, unrealistic? Call it what you want, ultimately, it's what we're all looking for, isn't it? A 'job' that allows us to enjoy the 'every day'. Love what you do, and you'll never work a day in your life, and all that jazz. It takes hard work to get there, as KB found out, but this should not deter anyone from holding on to that blue sky thinking that one day, they'll be able to turn up for work, whatever that 'work' looks like, with a smile on their face that sticks around all day. There will always be 'down' days, no matter how much you love the business and the things that you do, or make or provide, but the key to enjoying what you do is striving for more happiness than stress, more freedom than restriction. It doesn't have to be perfect, but you need to enjoy it. That's the journey and the destination, by the way.

COMMENTARY - A WORD FROM ADAM DAVISON

"As soon as we met and began talking, I realised we had many shared values and beliefs borne out of dealing with our own personal challenges that life had hurled at us over the last decade.

It isn't a case of sink or swim to me though. Rather it's all about the clarity of what you want to do differently and finding a way to achieve that. These major life changes do adversely affect some people but in my experience they build-up resilience in the majority. The resilience to deal with new adversity. I am reminded of the famous poem by Rudyard Kipling…"

"If you can keep your head when all about you

Are losing theirs and blaming it on you…"

3

THE ONE WITH THE TRAVEL ADVISOR. "A CULTURE OF GOOD"

We couldn't start a piece about a travel advisor without mentioning the coronavirus pandemic, which has obviously had a monumental impact on everyone involved within the industry, not least travel advisors like our third 'woman in business'.

However, we're going to take a leaf out of her book and talk about the positives of her journey to a successful business, rather than choosing to dwell on the challenges and struggles of the pandemic and everything that goes with it.

We all know about that already.

What we don't know yet, is what inspired a lady who had always wanted to be in the police force, to go into the travel industry, so let's find out.

LR has, by her own admission, always had a passion for travel, but only bought her franchise a little over three years ago, following a varied and sometimes very exciting employment history.

Having had her childhood dreams of being in the police force quashed on medical grounds, she embarked on a career in customs. So, there's always been some element of travel in her working life at least!

This was a role she loved, that eventually took her into the world of criminal investigations, joint intelligence and covert surveillance. It all sounds very exciting, but as soon as LR became a mother for the first time, the role just didn't fit with her priorities anymore.

So many women find that the world of business, whichever field they go into, provides so much more flexibility when starting a family or raising children. It's something that doesn't necessarily seem to make sense, when you consider the maternity pay and conditions that come with employment, but anecdotally, the flexibility of being a 'woman in business' and a mother, seems to work better than being an employee and a mother.

There will be differences of opinion on this of course, but no one is better qualified to give their opinion on this subject that someone who has seen it from both sides, and LR is one such person.

So, stepping away from the serious side of things for a moment, coronavirus and motherhood, what are the perks and pitfalls of a career in the travel industry? Is it as glamorous as people expect it to be?

LR has travelled the world in her role as a travel advisor, visiting a huge range of locations and sampling the delights of destinations from some of the farthest flung corners of our continents.

She has travelled all over America, including a stint in the 'back and beyond of Florida', visited Lapland, experienced luxury travel in continental Europe and even trekked through the jungles of Columbia, but it hasn't all been about indulging in the perks of travel just for herself.

Whether you believe it or not, this is all 'work' for her, and whilst LR accepts that she is fortunate to be able to 'nip from St Lucia to Antigua' for a night, she also makes it clear that the role is tiring and demanding. If she wasn't prepared to put the leg work in, exploring hotels and asking the right questions, LR would never be able to build the knowledge that her clients rely on.

And they really do rely on it.

Starting off with what LR calls 'more traditional' holidays, all inclusives and stag do/ hen parties, her business moved into the realm of creating tailor made packages for travellers looking for more of a bespoke holiday. And that's where the time spent travelling and talking really began to pay off for LR. Her level of expertise and experience outshines her competition, making her the obvious choice for her clients, who then refer her services to their networks in turn.

This is how she has built up her business – through hard work.

Whether or not you define travelling around the world as 'hard work' is up to you, but there is so much more that comes with the territory in her business, and she regularly pulls 'all nighters', just to make sure that her clients are safe, supported and satisfied with her service. It's hardcore travel and it's hardcore graft back in the office too.

All that time spent between hotel rooms and airport lounges has really paid off for LR, who saw the business turnover £1.5 million at the start of 2020. This made it clear to her that she had outgrown her franchise, and needed to go it alone, hence the formation of her own travel company, with LR becoming a fully independent travel advisor.

So, we've talked a little about why this business model works for LR, but why does it work in general? Why would anyone use a travel advisor when there are so many online travel companies?

It all comes down to 'choice paralysis', LR says, and the fact that there are simply too many options available to people these days. On average, people spend 38 hours over 8 nights looking at holidays online, and let's face it, they probably end up booking one of the first ones they looked at.

Consumers find their decisions influenced by things like reviews, good and bad, and it's all just a bit of an information overload, complete saturation. LR, and other advisors like her, act as the filter to all of this information. The choices are simplified based on her experience and knowledge, meaning that what she knows makes a big difference.

How does LR know all this again?

All that hard work spent travelling and looking in every nook and cranny of every possible location.

With a million and one questions from customers, those critical trips don't sound so much like a holiday any more...

The future of travel may not be certain at the time of writing, but her direction is crystal clear.

LR is acknowledging the route she has taken to this point in her business life, which is always important.

In this case, that's the support she has received as a franchisee, along with the education and opportunity that came with her decision to enter the industry in the first place.

But LR also has her mind set on where she's going, and as we've said before, that's even more important than where you've come from.

For LR, that means continuing to provide an unrivalled service and experience for her clients, keeping every part of her operation in line with her own ethos and beliefs. It also means further

growth, because with the level of dedication she has put into her business, growth is virtually a natural by-product...

...and speaking of virtually, we can't cover this 'woman in business', with all her positivity and optimism, without documenting a project they developed away from the business.

Wanting to create 'a culture of good', LR set up a virtual meeting hub, styled on a pub, named The Virtual Tavern, which at the time of writing has exceeded 40, 000 members. The hub has become a place for people to meet online, and a place that has been recognised for the positive impact it has had on the lives of so many during the global pandemic.

Do good things and good things come back to you. You get out what you put in.

These are simple ideas that have been written in a million different ways through the centuries, but for women in business like LR, they're more than just mantras, they're the key to success.

ANALYSIS & THEMES

Resilience – Without working on your resilience, you will fail in business. It's that simple. There are too many hurdles to jump over, too many mini failures to overcome and too much ruthlessness out there to accommodate those who lack resilience. It may seem harsh, it may sound unfair, but this is the stark reality of entering a highly competitive and at times, cruel world. LR showed resilience beyond belief during her battle to survive as a business throughout the coronavirus pandemic but survive she did. It would've been so much easier to abandon ship or cancel the flight, but she kept going. This was partly for her, but also for her clients, the people who have helped her build her business and the people to whom she feels immense responsibility. If you doubt your resilience, don't panic, this can be worked on.

Passion – You don't have to be a fanatic about something to make it succeed, but it helps. Toilet paper salesmen are probably not as passionate about their products as LR is about travel, for example, but they still need to bring passion of a fashion to their work. It might be a passion to solve a problem for consumers, or to provide a product that is unrivalled. It doesn't have to be a roaring passion for that actual product or specific service in a literal sense, but in LR's case, that's exactly what it was that got her into the business in the first place, and exactly what it is that fuels her to continue delivering an exceptional service to her clients. Passion, not fanaticism is the way forward, as with passion you can still see beyond your industry, you can still step away when you need to.

Hard Work – Never let anyone else's definition of 'hard work' convince you that your definition is wrong. It's human nature to believe that we have it harder than everyone else, or that certain industries and jobs require 'harder graft' than others, but it's all down to individual perception. Are we talking about physical struggle? In which case, it isn't fair to compare personal trainers with accountants. Are we talking about mental challenges? And perhaps this makes it unfair to switch the comparison around. But what does a personal trainer know about the accountant's day to day struggles? And to that end, what does the accountant know about the personal trainer's mental challenges? Absolutely nothing. Run your own race. LR has been running her own race from day one, and yes, irrespective of what anyone else thinks, it has been 'hard work'.

Do Other Stuff – Hobbies, pastimes, passions. Whatever it is that gets you going, be it sport, adventure, chilling out, make sure you give some time to it. Nurture your interests away from business. LR created an online hub for thousands of people to connect with each other. You don't need to do something as large scale as this, but 'doing other stuff', away from your business, is absolutely vital for anyone and everyone. If you're scratching your head and wondering exactly what it is that interests you, this advice is more important than ever. Step away from the business and find your hobbies, pastimes and passions away from the world of work. Step away from the coal face and allow yourself some 'quality time' doing the stuff that makes you tick.

COMMENTARY - A WORD FROM ADAM DAVISON

"What a conversation this was. It was a real case of knowing a person but then not knowing them at all.

Dig below the surface. Hear the back story. Realise the journey.

Then just go wow.

The whole fearlessness and idea of confronting things with the mindset to see the opportunity.

We have already talked about resilience and that is something you can see as a trait throughout all these stories.

That bouncebackability to stay on course in the teeth of a hurricane.

It also reminded me that you always need to understand the back story that everyone has in order to understand the person in front of you. Whether is a customer, suppler, employee or business acquaintance.

Take that time to listen. I mean really listen to them, and you gain so many more insights into who they are and with that information you can build a much stronger business relationship.

After all, isn't that what business is all about? Relationships?"

4

THE ONE WITH THE FRANCHISOR. "TO BE HONEST, I DIDN'T KNOW WHERE TO START"

Everyone's journey is unique to them, and whether they enter the world of business on purpose, by accident or even through necessity, the individual stories of how they got there are often what define a person's narrative and determines their success.

For CW, a former community nurse turned successful business owner, turned even more successful franchisor, the story of how she got there is just as important as the success she now enjoys.

CW loved her job as a district community nurse, something that was a vocation of sorts for her, as she came from a family of community nurses. Going into the family's traditional line of work is something that many people do, irrespective of gender, and we see it everywhere we look with 'Baker & Son' and 'Smith & Son' plastered over the backs of vans and the fronts of High Street shops across the country. For CW, it was a family vocation to 'care' and that's exactly what she did, delivering all kinds of care from wound dressing to palliative end of life services.

Now, whilst she was engaged in looking after her community, it's fair to say that CW had something on the back burner. In fact, she had this little something on the back burner for around five years. She had often become frustrated that she couldn't recommend a suitable home care provider for her patients. Not because she didn't know any, but because she didn't know any that she thought would be good enough to meet the needs and fulfil the requirements of the people she came into contact with.

Eventually, the lightbulb moment came to CW and she took the idea off the back burner and started to give it some serious consideration.

Instead of looking around for the solution to the problem, she decided that she would be the solution herself, and would set up a care business that ticked all the boxes she knew would be so essential.

Be the change you want to see, and all that.

The time at home for maternity leave afforded CW the time and space to formulate her plan.

The key question – 'What would I want to see if I was a patient?'

The answer to that question was easy for her, as she saw the needs of the community on a daily basis, and what's more, she understood them.

The tricky part of all this would be the business side of things, and by CW's own admission, she simply didn't know where to start.

She had absolutely no business background, yet she set about writing procedures, producing policies and creating a business plan. These are pretty shrewd steps for someone with no business experience, but it all came from a place of determination, fuelled by a willingness to learn as much as possible.

Now, this knowledge and knowhow wasn't accrued overnight, of course it wasn't, and it took her a great deal of time to be able to build what she calls 'the skeleton of a home care company'. Again, by her own admission, she probably did things the long way around, having

no idea about the type of help that was available, or even any idea of the existence of such a thing as a 'business coach...'

Nevertheless, she threw herself into things headfirst, spending five or six hours a night researching what to do next, how to do it, and crucially, why she needed to do it.

An obsession like this requires perfectionist tendencies, which is lucky for CW, as that's exactly what she has.

It took CW three years to get herself into a position from where the business was ready to trade, but she wasn't dragging her feet, she was putting as much as she could into ensuring that every box was ticked and that no stone was left unturned. Nothing less than 100% would've been acceptable for her, and her commitment was clearly bordering on the obsessive, but sometimes that's what it takes.

Amongst the biggest challenges when going to market, CW says that brand awareness was top of the list. Imagine spending three years on something and then no one knows anything about it, that's exactly what she was contending with.

50-to-60-hour weeks, building a business around a hectic job and building a family, it was never going to be easy, but nothing worth doing was ever easy, and CW stuck at it, 'totally winging it' at times.

Because of her meticulous planning (three years' worth) and her commitment to making the business a success, things took off in no time, and before two full years of trading were up, it was time to explore a new avenue – franchising.

But what is 'franchising?'

That's the question CW typed into Google after a suggestion from her accountant that she might want to explore her franchising options.

'That sounds about right' she remembers thinking, and that was that, back to the drawing board for the business.

Having to rewrite the paperwork and get all the legalities updated wasn't exactly ideal, but it was absolutely necessary for CW, who now spent time and money on outsourcing advice and assistance, though not always with the best results.

She found her franchising consultant to be ineffective but knows that this taught her a valuable lesson about who and where you get your help from.

Outsourcing, it turned out, as with bringing on new staff or selling franchises, is all about people, and the trouble with people is, well, they're people.

Fallible, flawed and with their own unique faults, people are difficult to deal with, it's a fact, but those who spend their time and energy finding the 'right' people, will always see the benefit in the long run.

The trick is to know who and what you're looking for, something that CW, as a franchisor, takes very seriously.

CW awarded 3 franchises within 6 months of exploring this new avenue but admits she could've awarded more. It all came down to the fundamentals of getting the right people in.

Brand reputation, and more importantly, client care, depended on it.

She now turns away more potential franchisee applications than she accepts, because if they're not right for the brand, they're not right for the brand.

With eleven up and running and two or three in the pipeline, the company now enjoys sustainable and steady growth, and the clients rely on the outstanding level of care they receive.

CW's love of learning continues, but she now educates others on franchising as well, as part of another of her businesses, a so called 'franchise school' for business owners looking to explore this avenue themselves.

A little bit like when she was a frustrated community nurse looking for a home care company to recommend to her patients, CW saw a lack of effective franchising consultancy, and used the old adage of 'if somethings worth doing properly, it's worth doing yourself'.

But surely, CW can't do it all herself. Surely, she isn't actually Superwoman.

No, she doesn't do it all herself, but she has invested more of her time, money and energy into finding the right team to work around her. The right people.

The key to CW's success, she reckons, is in her organisational skills, and whether it's business, personal or pleasure, everything is planned out to a tee, on a daily basis, to make sure it gets done.

It might have taken five years of thinking and three years of planning, but it's clear to see today, that anything CW decides has to 'get done', will ultimately, get done.

And it'll get done right.

ANALYSIS & THEMES

Be the Change You Want to See – Human beings like to moan, we're professionals at it in fact. We see problems and inefficiencies in all areas of the world around us, and from time to time, we mutter just how much better we could do things than they are currently being done. The truth of the matter though, is that whilst we like a moan, very few people are actually prepared to do something about it. They are not cut out to 'be the change they want to see', when actually doing something about our gripes and our moans, could present a brilliant opportunity to succeed in business. This is what CW found out, not once, but twice, as she created a care company to be proud of, and then a franchising school that makes a difference and does what it says on the tin.

Blag it – If you don't know what you're doing at times, don't worry, we've all been there. 'Blagging it' is not an excuse for poor knowledge or a lack of experience, but it is a necessary skill that all business owners must use on occasion. It's definitely not the key to success, but it really is a useful weapon to have in your armoury. There will always be things you don't know, and that's what we're here for, but in the heat of the moment, being able to 'totally wing it', as CW confesses to have done at times, is absolutely vital. Once you've successfully (or unsuccessfully) blagged something though, what should you do? Continue to blag it forever? No, you need to identify the gap in your knowledge or experience, and then do something about it. Book yourself on some training or seek the advice of someone in the know.

Do Your Research – At every single step in your business journey, doing the research is so important. In CW's story, we see a few examples of how research can work well and how it can potentially be done better. Do your market research in the beginning, spend a good deal of time on this. Research into your competitors and your potential customers will show you whether you have a viable idea in the first place. You also need to research the things you know nothing about. Park your ego at the door here and go back to school, or Google if you want a quick answer. A quick answer is exactly what CW got when she looked up what a franchise was, and now look at her. A little more research was needed when it came to employing the services of a consultant though, and she will have undoubtedly learned a valuable lesson from that.

Outsourcing – Your business is your baby, we get it, but there are times when it doesn't make sense for you to do absolutely everything associated with running the business. This is especially true when it comes to the things that other businesses are so skilled in, such as accountancy or legalities for example. Outsourcing is a necessity in business, but how do you know who to trust with your business, with your baby? Once again, it comes down to research and experience. There really is no substitute for experience, but even when things go wrong, mark it down as 'an experience' and learn from it. CW knows that time, money and stress were wasted on a 'bad experience' with outsourcing advice, but she turned it into a positive. Easier said than done, but doable all the same.

COMMENTARY - A WORD FROM ADAM DAVISON

"Follow a vision. That (to me) was the clear message from this conversation and that (to me) is one of the key things all new business owners must do.

If you set up a business and just keep your eye solely on the cash, then it is really unlikely to work. Not impossible, but definitely much harder.

Yes, I know running a business is about the bottom line, the money you can make, but when you are building something from scratch, that will only come if you have your vision. That picture in your mind. A picture not blurred, but so clear you can see the colours; feel the feelings it will give you.

You need this, as it will keep you going if and when the business doesn't quite go as you would like it to."

5

THE ONE WITH THE BUSINESS CONSULTANT . "A PATHOLOGICAL PROBLEM SOLVER"

Referring to oneself as a 'sales w****r' is not for everybody, but this particular, Northern wittish, brand of self-depreciation is not meant to shock in PD's case, only to serve as a reminder of where to draw the line between confidence and arrogance.

PD was, by her own admission, a bit of a 'sales w****r' back in the day.

Now, confidence, in the world of six figure salaries and posh German cars is key, but arrogance has a habit of hitting you where it hurts.

PD was confident, not arrogant, and that presented itself in a few surprising ways, like never being afraid to ask for help, yes that's right asking for help, a trait many people could benefit from.

Contrary to what a lot of people might think about the corporate world, asking for help in her company was seen as a great strength, rather than a sign of weakness. PD has tried to carry that ethos over into her life in business, but where did it all start for her?

As a highly driven and very successful, self-confessed 'corporate girl', PD could never have imagined stepping away from the security she enjoyed in the male dominated world of the industry she worked in. Always around the worlds of big banking and full-on finance, she was fascinated by pharmaceuticals and took a keen interest in how things operated.

Without realising it back then, she now knows that all of this was giving her the most amazing footing to be able to go into her own business...eventually.

Meeting her now husband changed everything, as romance often has a habit of doing.

PD's story is incredibly selfless, in that she knew she needed to make a change, not just for herself, but in order to help her husband find a way of earning a living that was not just sustainable financially, but also fulfilling creatively and artistically.

So, where would that change take her to?

Something related to the industry she worked in for so many years, big business or, at the very least, something with loose connections to the corporate world? That's what you'd think, and you'd be forgiven for doing so, but you'd be wrong.

Much to the surprise of those who knew her, including her boss, and probably to herself too, the change was a colossal shift into the world of beauty and cosmetics.

PD had always loved the personal care industry and was an avid user of things like facials and the latest permanent make up trends, but she was so much more in love with the results of these processes, than the processes themselves.

When visiting clinics and salons, she hated having to wait, and recalls how she regularly pulled apart the very foundations of the industry, whilst sitting in waiting rooms or on treatment chairs.

Why couldn't she come for a treatment on a Sunday?

Why did the music have to be so loud that she couldn't work on her laptop whilst receiving a treatment?

Why was there absolutely no flexibility within this industry?

PD admits that feeling as though she could 'do it better' might have been teetering into the realms of arrogance, but a few years down the line, she knows she was right.

A self-confessed 'pathological problem solver', she had always been driven mad by the inefficiencies and ineffectiveness of certain elements within the beauty industry. She felt a constant frustration with the lack of flexibility and, ultimately, felt as though clinics were simply not run properly.

The notion that she could do any better (never mind a lot better) seems a little unrealistic with hindsight, given that she couldn't even paint her own toenails, but the dream of owning a salon or beauty clinic endured. The idea wasn't going away. With her husband sacked from yet another call centre job, for being 'too nice', it was time to put her money where her mouth was and give this thing a go.

Now, we would always highlight the benefits of planning things carefully, over simply waiting for good luck to strike, but sometimes, serendipity is waiting just around the corner, and when PD took her husband to watch her getting her lips tattooed, serendipity did its thing.

An artist and tattooed person himself, her husband fell in love with the whole process, and whilst exploring their options for his next career move, the £14,000 course in body art seemed a relative bargain, coming in at a whole grand cheaper than going back to Uni. Bargain.

Now for PD to step across into the world of entrepreneurship, after all, as she remembers thinking, 'how hard can this be?'

At first, it was all a welcome distraction from the usual forecasts of the day job, applying the principals of her corporate world, to business ownership. PD set up a website, sorted out the sales funnels, and pretty much had the business structure all worked out, even before her husband had finished the course. Is this doing things back to front?

Not in PD's eyes, and we would absolutely back her when she claims that having the correct structure in place before launching, is one of the most important things you can do in business.

This wasn't just an investment financially, it was an investment in her partner's future, and in his happiness, and if that's not worth doing right, we don't really know what is.

She stepped out of the six-figure salary, away from the financial security and out of the posh German car, into a new world of business ownership, dealing with people.

And that's what a lot of people forget, PD now tells us with her business consultant head on (and don't worry we'll get to that bit), that business is about dealing with other people. And it's because of that fact, that new business owners must park their egos at the door.

That was pretty tough for a highly driven and hugely confident person like PD to do, but she knew they needed to, and the best way of giving this a head start was to employ the services of a coach, which is exactly what she did.

PD's advice about getting a coach is brilliant, and it's probably part of the reason as to why she's such a successful business consultant these days.

She says that in order for your relationship with a coach to be a beneficial one, you must find a coach who shares your ethos, and with whose values you find alignment. It doesn't have to be about 'the universe' or about certain mind sets, unless of course that's where you find your inspiration, but it's crucial that you find a coach who is singing from the same hymn sheet as you, or one who's singing from a hymn sheet that you'd like to be singing from one day.

Remember what we said about asking for help, that's what PD was doing, because as good as she was at selling storage systems to banks, she still couldn't paint her own nails and wasn't as clued up as she'd have liked to be about getting clients through the door to have their eyebrows tattooed.

Coming from a culture of success, where asking for help is not viewed as a weakness, but as a strength, saw PD in good stead to be able to absorb the advice her coach gave her, and then to implement it for herself, her husband and for their business.

If you don't ask for help, you're limiting your opportunity for growth, and that's the opposite of what PD has always been about.

She found power in simply being herself, from being mistaken for the waitress at presentations she was about to give, to dressing however she felt for meetings, rather than how she was perhaps expected to dress. At every single stage, success doesn't necessarily present as people think it should present.

This is straight from the PD brand of business consultancy here, but it's not about the material things, like who has the biggest car, or who has the flashiest watch. It's about finding your freedom and living the life you want to live. And yes, sometimes, change is the only way that we can begin to achieve that.

Fortunately for PD, she loves change, almost as much as she loves a challenge, and when she saw her global accounts take a nosedive in the wake of Brexit, PD was faced with a challenge like never before. It all felt a bit out of her control, and she remembers longing for redundancy, as at least that would take the decision out of her hands.

No redundancy would ever be likely to come for someone as valuable to the corporate world as she was, and so she needed to jump all on her own. Absolute madness, some people thought, including her boss, but with respect and admiration for her bravery, they stood back and watched as she ditched the six-figure salary for the salon.

A difficult period followed, with PD and her husband finding themselves 'skint to the back teeth', selling jewellery and cancelling holidays, but the power was all theirs, as the decision had been all theirs.

It was a heady cocktail of confidence, taking control of a situation and trusting the process, all mixed up with a hint of serendipity, that saw PD and her husband make a great success of things, but the journey to that success is what inspired her to take yet another leap into the world of business consultancy.

Her experiences are incredible resources for those she advises, but it is how PD entered into and then responded to these experiences that really mark her out as inspiration to those who choose to work with her, as long as their ethos and visions align, of course.

She is without question, a pathological problem solver, but PD is so much more besides.

She is a risk taker. She is an innovator. She is a go getter. She is a grafter. She is an inspiration.

But (and perhaps above all) PD is also a 'woman in business' who would (and has) put it all on the line for love.

And who are we to say that there is any greater motivation to succeed in business than that?

ANALYSIS & THEMES

Sort the Structure Out – If you take care of the foundations, building the rest of the house (or the business) is always a much smoother process. PD built the structure of the business, even before her husband was qualified to deliver the service that customers would ultimately come for. Investing in things like a website, sales funnels and properly written up T & Cs might seem like rushing to the finish line, but it is anything but. In fact, without the proper structures in place, and we're talking policies and procedures here, as well as websites and branding, your business might not even make it to the start line, never mind the end goal. Take your time to get things right behind the scenes, even if you're an 'eager beaver' who's raring to get going.

The 'Right' Reasons – We all have unique motivations for wanting to go into business. It may be that we want to escape the 9 to 5. It may be because we want the freedom to spend more time with our families. It may be because we want to earn more money. Whatever the reasons for wanting to make it in business though, it's important that we are sure that they are the 'right reasons' for us. Sometimes, the right reasons for us might look like the wrong reasons to everyone else. This was certainly true in PD's case, as to the outside world it looked as though she was stepping away from a six-figure salary and a life of luxury, into an unknown venture she had little to no experience in. It looked like a massive risk. That's exactly what it was, but PD's reasons were 'right' for her, in that she wanted to make the change for her husband. She wanted to help him find his calling and to experience fulfilment. The 'right' reason for her indeed.

Challenge Perceptions – One size very rarely fits all, this is especially true in the world of business. Just because suits, ties and formalities have been the main stay for a hundred years or more, does this mean we should keep up the tradition indefinitely? Maybe, that's up for you to decide, but if it doesn't sit right with you and your personality, challenge it. For women in business, this is so important, and challenging perceptions of who they are supposed to be, in the eyes of everyone else, is key to moving things forward and journeying closer to equality in every sense of the word. PD was 'herself' in the corporate world, authentic and genuine, wearing jeans and a top at presentations she herself was delivering. She was often mistaken for a waitress (nothing wrong with being the waitress, of course) but took great amusement and pride in walking up to deliver the presentation, dressed exactly how she wanted to dress. Challenge perceptions to change them.

Get a Coach – You don't know what you don't know, that's what we always say. Fortunately, though, there are people out there who do know what you need to know. You can outsource, you can work as part of a team, but something else which can move you forward in business, is getting a coach. Again, it's about parking your ego at the door and looking for someone who has values that align with your own. Coaches keep you accountable, and if you find the right one, they can accelerate your journey to your goals, and then help you set the next targets for your business, targets that will make a difference to your professional life and your personal life. Oh, and guess what, even the coaches have coaches. So, do it, get a coach.

COMMENTARY – A WORD FROM ADAM DAVISON

"Occasionally in life you meet people that are just a force of nature. They exude an infectious energy that you feel when you are in their presence. And this was just one of those occasions.

The unlimited energy, the passion for the business, the conviction that what she was doing was the right thing, and the willingness to take a chance and then continue taking a chance in order to move forward and progress.

Standing still is never an option and the career jump from corporate world to small business owner clearly showed courage but also self-belief.

To have this level of self-belief is rare. So many people I come across in business have to deal with the anxiety of the decision before making the actual decision to go into business, but when they feel the fear and do it anyway, they soon realise that they can be successful.

They say the sky's the limit but there is a universe beyond the sky. It can feel really scary to look at the universe and think what you want, but you are only limited by your own beliefs."

6

THE ONE WITH THE RECRUITMENT SPECIALIST. "CANDIDATES AS POUND SIGNS AND NOT AS PEOPLE"

RM had been in recruitment, specifically IT recruitment, for a period of six and a half years, when she realised that the role, she was occupying was not exactly fulfilling her desire to truly help people. She found herself in the unusual position of working for a private company within the public sector, and without wanting to cause too much of a stir here, saw first-hand just how much money, taxpayer's money at that, was routinely wasted on projects that never came to be.

To say that RM felt frustrated would be something of an understatement.

The corporate world of recruitment was always interesting for her, but in 2017 RM took the leap away from a career, into the world of being self-employed. The adventure began.

Certain things had changed in her employment circumstances, and without wanting to go in to too much detail over it, political decisions on a national scale had her feeling as though she was no longer on a level playing field with many other recruiters around her.

RM chose to leave, and the empowerment that came with that decision was tempered only ever so slightly by a new job, a job that she lasted in for the grand total of seven weeks. By her own admission, she hated this new job, and could've left after seven seconds, never mind seven weeks. Alas, out of necessity, her recruitment company was born.

Often seen as 'disruptive' in busy office environments, due to her personality and need to question everything (especially BS), RM was now prepared to go it alone. Well, sort of.

In many ways, 'going it alone' for her would feel like the exact opposite, given the emphasis she puts on the value of networking, when telling her story.

Even though becoming self-employed was never really on the radar for RM, she dropped a hint that she could still provide recruitment services, something she has always been passionate about, but that she would do it on her own terms and in her own way.

On her own terms and in her own way meant with absolutely no BS, something which even makes the tagline for her business.

As we're always keen to point out to people, you really are your business, meaning that it is so important to marry up your personal ethos and attitudes, with that of your business, whatever they may be. For RM, this meant placing a huge amount of importance on open and honest conversations. They are what make her tick. No faffing around, no messing, just getting straight to the nitty gritty of a role or recruitment matter.

One of the main reasons for her success in business, and as an entrepreneur, has to be down to just how genuine she is. What you see really is what you get, and in business, that level of genuineness is hard to find. Not only that, but it's also priceless.

RM cannot and will not ever pretend to be someone she isn't (apart from in her acting gig, but more on that later) and it is her honesty and straightforwardness which stand her out as someone who clients and candidates want to work with.

She sees her role as vital to the candidates she looks to match up with a range of positions, knowing that her work is contributing not just to their professional lives, but also to their personal worlds.

Needing to 'paint a picture,' for the candidate is how RM describes the situation, and she is keen to state that in an interview and on boarding situation, employers are being interviewed by candidates as much as the other way around. This candidate driven approach is at odds with a large percentage of the industry, who perhaps view candidates as pound signs and not people, something which she sees as fundamentally wrong.

RM is a 'people person' in the truest sense, and pins her successes on the effectiveness of networking. Networking in a structured and professional environment is beneficial for all businesses, and we would advise any business owner to make a concerted effort to at least give it a go. RM's experiences are profoundly positive, but she is not alone in this.

It's slightly ironic since 'going it alone', that it seems to have been networking that has made the biggest difference to her business, in that she does not only recruit for IT companies now, but also for the range of businesses she networks with.

A non-exhaustive, 'off the top of the head' type list, includes recruitment for accountants, electricians, kitchen designers and sales staff, but as long as the IT sector manages to evade any kind of 'dip' it will remain the bread and butter of the business. The 'bread and the butter' of the business is very important, but it's not always what business owners want to get out of their self-employed life. RM has never chased the money though and says that as long as she covers her bills and is able to lead what she calls 'a nice life', she's happy.

Recruitment is about getting the right people into the right positions at the right time, no mean feat, and that means putting people first. Listening to RM, you can really hear her love of people come across, and it's easy to see how she embraces networking to further her own business, but also to help other peoples' businesses, other people who have adopted the self-employed life for similar reasons to her.

So, what else does this hard working, person focused woman get up to?

Well, considering she talks about herself as someone who can't do two things at once, the answer might surprise you. With all the additional time she freed up after escaping the corporate rat race, she has been able to take on not just one, but two and even three extra roles, all whilst continuing to operate her outstanding recruitment business.

Amongst the other strings to her bow, are her responsibilities as a utilities services provider, working on behalf of a growing company who look to make peoples' lives easier with just one all overarching utilities bill. She is also a representative for a company who design and supply Digital Business Cards, something she says are 'the future' and offer so much more than a traditional business card. They offer a whole marketing platform, and work either instead of or alongside a website.

Finally (for now anyway) RM works for a casting agency as an extra, appearing in household TV programmes in and around the background.

That's about the only place you'll ever see this businesswoman pretending to be something she isn't.

Business without the bull indeed.

ANALYSIS & THEMES

Networking – Networking is the magic ingredient to those who use it well, and a 'complete waste of time' to those who use it incorrectly. Having a reliable network around you, filled with people you 'know, like and trust' can be like having your own personal sales team working for you, even when they're not with you. RM swears by her network, and regularly sees the benefits of working alongside professionals from a wide range of disciplines, from tradespeople to accountants and solicitors. It can be scary at first, the idea of putting yourself and your business 'out there' for all to see, but once you've found the right place, the right people and the right purpose, a network will stand you in good stead to succeed. There is one caveat with all of this though, that RM knows well, you have to put in as much as you are expecting to get out. That's the beauty of a good network, it is symbiotic.

People First – In business, it is so easy to get bogged down in the numbers and the paperwork that we forget that successful business depends on one thing, people. The people you work with, the people you provide a service or a product to, 'you' as well. We're all of us, just people, and having a 'people first' approach to your business life is vitally important. RM said that they didn't want to see candidates as pound signs, but as people, and that's the approach we should all be taking. If you see the customer as an individual, or as part of a well-established group identified by things such as age, gender and interests, then you give yourself the advantage when it comes to identifying your customer avatar. You have to understand people first, before they will bring you a profit. The key to all this? Relationships, relationships, relationships. Build them. Develop them. Nurture them.

Know What You Want – You might be driven by the money, and that's absolutely fine, as long as you know that's what you want. This is less to do with business goals, and more to do with our own intrinsic motivations. RM was happy to admit that she wanted to earn enough money to pay the bills and lead a 'nice life', because her ultimate goal was to provide a quality service for candidates going into new roles. Obviously, this was in addition to serving her clients, but is further proof of her 'people first' approach. By knowing what she wants out of business, she puts herself in a better position to, firstly, be able to achieve that and, secondly, actually enjoy the process of getting there. This isn't to say that wanting to earn big bucks is wrong, that's absolutely fine if that's what you want. Just make sure you know what you want.

Be Versatile – As long as you can keep the plates spinning, there is nothing wrong with being versatile. Multitasking is not solely for women as the myth would have you believe, but it just so happens that many women in business are excellent multi taskers anyway. This series of stories shows you the real-life accounts of highly successful businesswomen, who are also devoted mothers, loving partners and caring individuals who make an active contribution to society away from the world of business. RM used to have herself down as someone who couldn't do more than one thing at once, but even a quick glance at her journey shows just how much a person can do at once, if they manage their time accordingly and are able to cope with the pressures associated with taking on a few different roles at once. Conquer versatility, and the world is your oyster. To the victor, the spoils.

COMMENTARY - A WORD FROM ADAM DAVISON

"We all know that one person who is really grounded in life, calls 'a spade a spade' and just knows the direction they want.

Refreshing to hear such clarity and also the desire to focus on people and not just the fact that they are a commodity to be placed, and to bring in a fee.

I think many people in small businesses actually miss this one.

They leave the corporate world to set up in business because they don't like being treated like a number!

They set up a business. They employ staff. And then treat them like a number or even forget that their customers are people too and want to be treated in a particular way.

I have seen it so many times but really the people do come first!

All small business owners should every so often take a look at their business viewed from their customers or employee's eyes.

Try it. Do you like what you see?

7

THE ONE WITH THE TRAINING CONSULTANT. "IT ALL FALLS ON YOU!"

Everything starts and ends with you. This is so true in the world of the small business owner, but at times, we fail to give this the understanding and respect it truly deserves, which is something that LM struggled with before setting up in business on her own, and for some time afterwards as well.

Now a busy HR and training consultant, LM set up in business on her own to try and redefine her work/ life balance, which she admits was all out of whack in the world of employment.

Initially, she didn't make the full leap, but remained in place on a part time basis, whilst trying to establish her new business and, as she puts it, find her feet.

It took a toll on her own personal mental health, the constant pressure to perform, but with everything under your own remit, it can be difficult to not get sucked in to replying to just one more email or allowing yourself to answer just one more call.

With this experience under her belt of transitioning from the world of work to self-employed status, via a brief dalliance with a bit of both, she is now well positioned to help others who find themselves in a bit of a similar situation, which is why she runs Mental Health First Aid courses, on top of her training consultancy business.

Business owners are notoriously bad at looking after themselves mentally, but she knows that you absolutely must look after you, because nobody else will.

Mental health is coming to the forefront more and more with each passing year, sometimes because of worrying trends like an increase in suicide rates, and sometimes because of more positive occurrences like public campaigns.

No one wants to hear of even one person losing their life to suicide, as a result of a battle with their mental health, but it is a twenty first century issue we all must face. Resilient, hardworking, successful business owners are not immune from the pressures of modern life, both the professional and the personal, and can be just as susceptible to the internal battles we all face on a daily basis.

"Am I good enough?"

"Will I succeed?"

"What if I fail?"

How many business owners out there have had to face up to those questions in the last twelve months, or in the last twelve minutes even?

We'd bet it's a lot, if not most of them.

LM's popular courses help business owners find a way to 'turn off' these lingering questions, and to look after themselves mentally, so that they can perform as well as they would like to in business.

Speaking of performance then, and harking back to her own business, away from the Mental Health side of things, what exactly is it, that makes an employee engage with the vision of a company and perform more efficiently and effectively?

It isn't policies and procedures, that's for sure, and even though she can help businesses with this always necessary but often-times laborious side of things, it is with another angle that she finds the most enjoyment.

It isn't rocket science - highly engaged employees perform better than under engaged employees, but many employers are so close to the coal face that they can't see the opportunities they're missing.

This is where LM comes in, with her knowledge and knowhow of how to get the very best out of the people who work for the people she works for.

It's a bit of a mouthful if you say it quickly, but break it down and it makes perfect sense...

LM helps the employers she works with find ways to get the best out of the people that work for them.

This means incentives, rewards, projects, shared responsibilities...

The list is endless and open to expansion and innovation, two things she is always keen to 'go big' on with her clients.

Many companies, we know, see HR and training consultancy as an expense rather than an investment, but looking after your people will always benefit the business in the long run.

Just as looking after yourself, as a business owner, will benefit you, the business and everyone around you too.

So, HR and training then, they really aren't two things that small businesses can afford to just pay lip service to. They must be taken seriously, worked on regularly, pulled apart, analysed, reviewed and revamped. LM knows this, and she shows businesses how to do it, but more importantly perhaps, she shows business owners how to look after Number One.

You are life's essential element. You are your business. Don't forget that.

ANALYSIS & THEMES

Investment vs Expense – In business, you simply have to know the difference between an investment and an expense. Especially in the early days of setting up in business, every single pound you spend can feel like an expense, but this couldn't be further from the truth, as long as you have confidence in where the money is going. In LM's story, she talks about the value of good HR and good incentives for staff, because she has seen first-hand what a difference they can make. But the conflict between investments and expenses is far reaching, and businesses of all kinds play out a daily battle between spending and skimping. Outsource when you need to but do your research in advance. Budget for training and development, because a lifelong commitment to learning is crucial to success. Retrain your mind set, because sometimes, you really do have to speculate to accumulate, and with the right advice, speculation is never a gamble.

Be Kind – Simplistic? Yes. Necessary? Absolutely. Business has long been regarded as a 'cutthroat' environment or a 'dog eat dog' world, and with good reason too. Sometimes, business is a confrontational, scary domain to operate in, especially if you're brand new, but does this mean we should forget the importance of such a simple message as being kind? We don't think so, and it's clear from LM's story that we should make no apologies for being kind, in everything that we do. The reality is, that none of us really know what is going on in anyone's personal life, and that we can't be aware of the different challenges we each face. So, yes, there will be deadlines and deals that need to be discussed. Yes, there will be disputes and disagreements that need to be dealt with. But, and it's a big 'but', kindness can still be present in all that you do. It is so important.

Mental Health Awareness – It isn't just a buzz term thrown around to gain a few brownie points. Mental health awareness is finally receiving the respect that it deserves, in society in general that is, not just in business. As business owners and people working within business, we have a responsibility to acknowledge the impact that working in a stressful environment, especially during uncertain times, can have on a person's mental health. Never underestimate the way different things impact on different people. Everyone reacts differently to everything, and we should do our best to show patience and understanding with everyone we come into contact with, however challenging that may be. Signposting people to the appropriate channels of help, such as the Mental Health First Aid courses mentioned in LM's story, is a very useful thing to do.

YALEE – You are life's essential element. It's no use being kind if you're not kind to yourself. It's no use being aware of everyone else's mental health, if you forget to look after your own. Wherever possible, you should always give yourself the breathing space you need to be able to refresh, reflect and reset. This might mean turning off the phone and setting the 'out of office' on your emails at a certain time each night. This might mean scheduling a day or two every month, just for you, to do something that you love. However, you practice 'self-care', make sure you do it well and often, because without you, there can be no business.

COMMENTARY - A WORD FROM ADAM DAVISON

"In the last few years, the awareness of mental health has really increased. Mental health first aiders are more and more common in large businesses yet for so many small business owners it is put firmly in the back seat.

"I haven't got time for that."

A common phrase many tell themselves.

Well, small businesses are an extension of the people who set them up. Have a healthy mind, body and soul and you will be much better placed to grow and develop your business.

This conversation reminded me that it is so critical to take time for you. This isn't a cost, it's an investment. An investment that will pay dividends in the long term."

CONCLUSION

Women in business, that's how it's done.

A variety of stories that highlight the trials and tribulations, as well as the successes, of a number of inspiring businesspeople, who happen to be women.

The inequalities and prejudices faced by women in business will not disappear overnight, and it is our responsibility to continue to shine a light on the reality of their stories.

They do not succeed despite the fact they are women. In many cases they succeed because they are women and, in most cases, it is altogether irrelevant.

The themes which we extract from their stories are themes that are found across the world of business, irrespective of gender.

It is hoped that by detailing these stories, as we have done in this book, the first volume of a series, we will inspire women and girls to want to explore their options for going into business.

Creativity and ingenuity are the prerequisites. You already have those.

Hard work and resilience are the tools to get you started. These can be developed over time.

Advice and guidance are the key ingredients for getting you where you want to go. After all, you don't know what you don't know, and that's where we come in.

Success and happiness are the rewards.

So, over to you...

Printed in Great Britain
by Amazon